The New Christian Whatever

Dialogues About Important Jesus Stuff

BEN DONLEY

Jock and Lola Publishing

Copyright © 2014

Designed by S. J. Forester
Cover by Randall Fuller

Printed in the United States of America

ISBN-13: 978-1-940816-02-9
ISBN-10: 1-940816-02-5

Dedicated to those who want to
be hardcore followers of Jesus but
who still really suck at it . . .

The New Christian Whatever: Dialogues

This book is filled with short essays about Christian issues that have been rattling around in my spirit and mind for many years. As you will see, each essay is followed by a set of formative questions, which will hopefully help you process and react practically to the words I wrote. If certain essays piss you off or offend your sensitivities, I am sorry.

Actually I take back my pre-apology, because you probably need to be challenged by someone who has had his butt kicked by life, church, and ministry for over fifteen years. Most of us spoiled brat Christians need to be spurred on toward love and good deeds on a regular basis.

So, read at your own risk.

Anyway, I do hope this book challenges you to have deep dialogues with one another and that your walk with Jesus Christ deepens. We are all in this together and we all need each other to press on through an annoying world. Thanks for reading and please be looking for the second installment of *The New Christian Whatever Series* coming soon to an e-bookstore near you.

Table of Contents

Kick Ass Jesus?

I want the Omega—not the Alpha.

The beginning was cool. The manger was fine. And the baby was probably cute.

But I can hardly stand fixing my eyes on the Christmas settings. I do not want to get stuck at the first breaths of a gurgling savior.

I want to move forward and past the dirty birthplace and even beyond the empty tomb.

I want my mind on the Jesus of Revelation—the kick ass Jesus.

The blazing, fiery flashlight face Jesus. The One who is yet to come to put an end to the suffering, to stop the tears and the groaning of a world falling apart.

The Jesus who will be responsible for making all things new and probably knows jujitsu. The powerful rider who has the keys I need.

The Jesus who conquers.

Forget the star. Forget the shepherds. Forget the baby who got his umbilical cord cut and who pooped in some sort of diapers.

I do not want to bow down next to a brave baby.

I don't want to think about his first 12 years.

I want to throw my crowns down at the feet of the sword-mouthed world renovator.

Give me the one who will come again. The one who will show up across the entire sky and cannot be denied by anyone.

Can we have a sweet holiday dedicated to this version of our Jesus? We could wear halogen lights and dye our hair white and paint our faces pale.

We could lie down in our yards and watch for the new city to drop down from the sky: the city to replace all human kingdoms (even America).

You see, cute has been done, and I am done with it. I am thankful for the manger and beyond thankful for the cross; I am glad there was a great beginning, but hit me with some Omega God.

Send the End into our skies and rule us.

December 25th to me is Christ-was.

But I want Christ-is.

Don't you?

Q & A:

—What images immediately pop into your mind when you think about Jesus?

—Do you think it matters how you "picture" Jesus when you pray, seek him, consider him?

—Do you think there is an over-emphasis on the "Talladega Nights" Jesus (aka Lord Baby Jesus in his ghost manger)? Or on the "Passion of the Christ" Jesus (aka Beaten/Crucified Jesus)?

—Why do you think people tend to focus on the earthly versions of who Jesus was rather than on who he is now?

—What does it mean to have a Lord who overcomes?

—What does it mean to be an Overcomer (practically)?

—What do you imagine your glorious body will be like? Are you excited to receive it? Are you happy that you won't need to do CrossFit to keep it in shape?

—What does it mean to be prepared for Jesus's return? How are you readying yourself on a daily basis?

—What are the biggest distractions/hindrances to focusing on the realities of the spiritual?

When Life Falls Apart

I've learned to stop asking God two types of questions.

　　　　Why? and How long?

I used to arrogantly and foolishly interrogate God with variations of these two questions, but now they are absolutely off limits, even when my desires and emotions insist on being dosed with satisfactory answers. After what I've gone through for three years, I have most sensibly taken off my watch, ceased looking for the waiting room door to open, and forced my tongue to go silent—to quit asking why things are and are not happening to me.

"Are we there yet?"

"Why is *my happiest life now* so bad when I'm all Jabez'ed-up?"

Who cares? The simple truth is that God's ways are higher than mine.

And not just a little higher than mine. His ways are Immeasurably Higher. And honestly, I don't think I would be able to handle His reasons anyway if they did not match my selfish and spoiled expectations. If God revealed a twenty-ycar plan when I was hoping for a three-month one, I might fire assault weapons at the sky, build a golden iPad to worship, or scream challenges at my Maker for a Jacob-style MMA match.

How did I get to this place?

I can assure you it was not a deep exegetical study of the book of Job that altered my wondering ways. Instead, it was my own life that buried those questions. A life committed to Jesus. A life completely dedicated to a direct calling into professional ministry. A life broken into a billion parts in just twenty-four months by a loving Father who was not going to stand for my self-hating, performance-driven, perfectionist-proving, self-righteous and charismatic glory-grabbing any longer. It was love but a very painful kind.

Here's a brief account: after a combined fifteen years of doing missionary work in Asia, reaching out as an Urban Pastor to the drug addicted and mentally ill in LA, fighting for social justice in DC, trying my hardest to make a spiritual and overall transformative difference in the lives of the American homeless, and preaching, teaching, doing discipleship and a lot of counseling within several different churches, I mentally and emotionally crashed—hurtling myself at 250 mph into what felt like an electrified steel wall covered in barbed wire. The confident rising star for the Kingdom became wreckage fired into a black hole.

Seemingly overnight, the go-to pastor, must-see counselor, creative church consultant, and *hilarious* but truth-telling preacher everyone wanted to hear, became a paralyzed, fetal-positioned, couch-drenching tear gusher with a nervous system acting out in total rebellion. I was broken by serious clinical depression and severe anxiety that could not be prayed or even Xanaxed away.

Hour after hour. Day after day. Month after month.

"Why is this happening to me?" "When is this going to end?"

I spent long periods praying out in soul-poverty and self-pity. I got very friendly with Elijah as he asked for God to kill him rather than allow his struggle to continue. I seriously considered walking in front of a speeding bus, because I was too weak to go on with life. I had been raised by a culture that taught me to be surprised by the pain of God's good discipline. I was unaccustomed to anything so harsh as this—I had been to Seminary but had never taken the prerequisite courses in basic Christian struggle.

During those three years, a ton happened. But here is a quick summary of God's grace amidst my ruin: Jesus actually placed His comforting hand on my cheek one night just as I was ready to turn in my timecard. He told me to breathe and to stop trying so hard; the Father destroyed my pastoral facade, stole my self-hate, and made me into someone I like; the Holy Spirit ruined my popular messages but told me I finally had something worthwhile to speak about to a population of my fellow depressed and brokenhearted.

Overall, God saved me from me.

"I will rejoice because You have rescued me. I will sing to the Lord because He is good to me." Psalm 13:5-6

Q & A

—Have you ever had your life altered in such a way that you were not able to recognize yourself afterward?

—How did you react emotionally? Mentally? Spiritually?

—Do you ever find yourself putting a timer on God (begging Him to tell you how much longer something is going to last)? Has it ever helped you?

—Why do you think God makes us wait on His movement and His help?

—Can you identify with David's very real struggles in any areas of your life? Are you able to just trust without questioning God's timing or His reasons?

—Why ask "why" to God?

—When you don't get what you want or need within a certain time frame, how do you typically react? Do you tend to try to find your own way out?

—When have you ever felt that God was being unfair to you? That He was being too slow? That He was ignoring you?

Close to me

I cannot get this one picture out of my head: The prodigal son is being embraced by his father after living a long time as a wasteful idiot in a distant country (see verses in Luke 15:11-31).

Here is what blows my mind the most.

Near the end of the story, the prodigal son returns home from a life of waste and disgust. He stinks of pigs and sweat even before he begins his journey home.

Since he comes from a distant country, you can imagine the increase of stink and dirt as he makes the trip back with only his two feet. He had no Motel 6 to stop into on the way home—no Greyhound bus to rush him there faster.

He had no place to freshen up.

When he got near enough to home that his father saw him, I imagine that his father could also smell him from far away.

The scent of a prodigal, a man who misses the mark by a mile, trudging home in shredded clothes with head down probably holding his own nose.

And then, when the father approached him with his old running legs and stood face to face with him, he did not wait until his son could get a much-needed shower. He did not spray Febreze all over him. He did not order that a bath be drawn. He did not throw his arms around him while holding his breath. He just brought him near. He had no disgust for the dirt or the grime built up over this distant journey home. He showed that his love was the sort that is quick to swallow up the distance and certain enough to ignore the vile stench.

With one act, the father took his son from as far away to as close as possible—there was no space between clean father and dirty child. The father showed his son that he was willing to carry the lingering smells of lostness and death.

This might be my favorite part of the Prodigal story.

No shower. The B.O. is super-sized. But the father embraces his child and kisses him on his sweaty cheek nonetheless.

This is our God.

And we need to receive His love today, this kind of unshowered love.

As we all return to His presence today after covering some kind of ugly distance needing a shower (using a blend of jojoba shampoo and pure Dove soap), understand that He will grab you before you can go there.

He is a God who gets dirty to bring us back to life. He is a God who stoops down to make us great.

When He comes to you today, reach out your arms and let Him remind you that you are His loved child. Do not try and hold Him at arms' length because you have overwhelmed your spiritual deodorant and are embarrassed by the proof of your pigsty.

Say it with me: "God, I stink today. Thanks for not caring about that as much as you care about my sonship."

As for me, it is good to be near God.

How about you?

Q & A

—What have been your "distant countries" relative to God's house? What was it like to be so far away? So far apart?

—Do you still own "timeshares in Sodom" that you keep for rainy days? In other words, are you all the way home, or are parts of you still allowed to escape into distant apart-ments?

—Why do you run from safety and fullness to insecurity and famine?

—Have you ever been brought into absolute closeness with God? What was it like?

—Would you ever allow another human being to wrap his arms around you when you were sweaty, stinky, and disgusting? Or would you keep him at arms' length and warn him against your grossness? Why or why not?

—After debasing yourself with the world's vices, do you try to "clean up" before you reach out to God?

—How do you feel about God's taking you into His closeness when you are at your worst?

—What keeps you at arms' length from God?

A Mind is a Terrible Thing to Waste

I went to school from age 4 to age 26. That is 20-plus years of education. And I am not a slacker. I paid attention. I was there for the majority of days. I took notes. I got my high school diploma with honors. I got my double major and my Masters with Summa Cum Laude recognition. But it was mostly a waste of time.

Here is what my education has taught me:

-Progress is best—even if it kills a lot of people.

-Busyness is a virtue as is speed.

-Solitude and Silence are punishments.

-Money is god. It makes the world go around. In money we trust.

-I am responsible for providing for myself and my family.

-Truth tellers get murdered. (Socrates, Jesus, Gandhi, Martin Luther King, Jr.)

-Truth is applauded until applied.

-Success is accomplishing the American Dream.

-Failure means that I did not accomplish the American Dream.

-Everyone should be educated and well-rounded.

-Self-defense justifies everything.

-The Constitution is the final word (even if it originally treated African-Americans and women as inferior).

-Tolerance is best.

-Voting is the best way to be heard. It is a duty.

-Be selfish and our greed will ultimately trickle down to others.

-The most dangerous people are those who are different from me.

-Bread and Circus always tame the masses.

-The Declaration of Independence is great unless used as a justification for revolt against this nation.

-I was randomly and accidentally made.

-There are acceptable and unacceptable addictions.

-We=Civilization.

-Non-conformity is punished.

-"Terrorists" are those who disagree with *my world* so much that they try to destroy it.

-"Patriots" are those who disagree with *my enemies' worlds* so much that they try to destroy it.

-Having your own kids is a big deal that everyone should strive for.

-Ugly people, stupid people, and old people are candidates for rejection.

-The greatest artists are ignored until after they are dead.

-That Des Moines is the capital of Iowa.

-$2 + 2 = 4$.

-Grade D meat equals a Happy Meal.

-Change is accepted if it makes a lot of the "right" people a lot of money.

-30,000 far-off people dying everyday is an acceptable number.

-Death and taxes only half applies to the rich.

-Medicine makes us well.

-Doctors know what they are talking about.

-At funerals, everybody goes to Heaven.

-If you do leave the cave, it is better to stay quiet when you come back inside.

-Senior Pastors must give the main sermon, even if they are terrible speakers.

-Technology is wonderful.

-At 65, you are no longer needed in the workplace and should retire.

-Homeless people are to be avoided—they have failed and are probably contagious.

-Luxury cars prove something great about their owners.

-Great movies make the least money.

-Middle class people can never be President.

-If I work hard, I can do anything I want.

-A college education will guarantee me a good job.

-Getting good grades at school is important.

-Say "no" to drugs.

-Sex with lots of people is the relational goal of most TV characters.

-I need a lot of new clothes. Style and Vanity are key.

-Celebrities are special people who deserve special treatment.

-A Harvard education (Ivy League) is better than State University Education.

-Blood is thicker than water.

-Darwin, a simple man, tapped into the truth about the beginnings of life and is only doubted by really stupid people.

-Church is for Sundays.

-The television must be used daily.

-Information is power.

-Award shows matter.

-Corporations rule the world.

-You can pull yourself out of the gutter if you work hard enough.

-America is the land of opportunity.

-Cheaters never win.

-Liars never prosper.

-Justice is blind.

-Diamonds are a girl's best friend.

*Some of the above is true. Much of it is false. But most of us are guided in our actions and decisions by both the true and the false. That's why so many people suffer.

We have been miseducated.

We have been misinformed.

We have been lied to.

We have been indoctrinated.

But if you mix in enough truth with the foolishness, mind control is easy to attain.

Q & A

—Have you ever been taught to think for yourself, or are you a memorizer of the status quo equations?

—Do you ever question what you have been taught, or are you an addict of expertise and certainty?

—How have you allowed culture to indoctrinate you? In what areas have you been "fed" information, and in what areas have you actually taken the time to check for the truth before swallowing it without question?

—How did Jesus use his wisdom to question the indoctrination of his times? How did the world and the religious react to it?

—How does "speaking the truth in love" translate to your every day dealings?

—When is it okay to move from "gentle redirections" to "woe be unto you snakes?"

Here Am I Lord, Send Him

God, I am your man.

I want the job.

That is, unless it is in Africa or in the Amazon.

Or really anywhere that begins with an A—

Antarctica, Alabama, Arkansas—no thank you.

I will allow Australia because I do love you, Lord.

Also I will go anywhere you say as long as anacondas are not present;

I do not understand why you made anacondas so large.

Roaches and wall-sized spiders are off limits, too -

Those I can do without.

But I would rather not do without television or warm water.

I think you wouldn't want me to suffer these losses. You are a God who gives blessing.

I will do anything that you ask—I will be your top volunteer as long as it pays me a decent salary and a 401-K.

A company car or a Missionary Volkswagen would be nice as well.

Oh yeah, and I do want to know how long this task will take—I don't want this open-ended commitment.

I do have things that I do want to accomplish for myself.

Truly, I am on board if it is fulfilling, and I get to see immediate rewards.

And comfort is a plus.

The people I go to need to know my language.

The food I eat there best not be too native.

Happiness is Happy Meals and some chicken from Kentucky in a neighborhood nearby.

And also, would you make this job impressive to those around me—I don't want any Henri Nouwen thing where I have to take care of one handicapped man. I do not want anyone out there thinking I am wasting my potential on wiping butts. I want some Billy Graham bling: the suit and tie and the adoring millions.

I am willing, don't you see?

I cannot imagine why I can't hear you calling...

I have so few exceptions,

So few conditions.

Just these:

> Keep me in America, not far from the middle class.

> Don't ask me to change, suffer, surrender, or die.

> How can I be any good to you dead?

How about you call me to stay right here on this leather couch eating these flaming hot Cheetos watching college basketball?

My family has to approve. My parents would freak if I live my life to raise support and work for orphans.

My wife has to want to go.

It has to be something I like and somewhere I love with an Apple Store within walking distance.

It can't be inner city.

It can't be outer village.

I have to have a cable computer connection,

constant email and download capabilities.

It'd better not be dirty, either.

The toilets have to be similar to those I have always used— I dare not squat over a tiny hole without Charmin or go in non-stalled public dumping grounds.

Lord, you had porcelain, too, didn't you?

Washer and dryer in house is a necessity.

Cell phone—necessity. Sports Center—necessity.

Really, God, to be honest, I think I am made to be a businessperson who makes millions and then glorifies you with it.

I want you to use my dreams;

I want you to use my major—at least my minor.

Send me on an errand that I am good at, something that shows off my skills.

Don't put me out there in a world where you use my weaknesses to give You glory.

Let me show off some.

It just doesn't make sense to me that you might place me somewhere that I go unknown,

where I might fail,

where no one gets saved,

where no one applauds me.

So, I am willing as long as the above is considered.

Thanks, God.

Let me know.

****

Willingness.

Why do I bring up all of this?

Because many of us say we are willing, but we are not.

Send me, God, we sing, but we go nowhere—why?

Why is it that we are not being sent?

Why is it that we are not being called?

Could it be that we have so many exceptions that when God has a job opening for a Kingdom work, he has to pass over our names because we allow so little room for movement?

I know I do not have the willingness.

I will admit it.

I want details from God first.

I want God to send me an editable itinerary letting me know the following:

Who, what, when, where, why, how, and how long?

Will I be paid well?

Will I be a success?

Can I still do my own thing?

Will I be able to rely on my strengths?

Will it be glamorous?

Will I like the people I am around?

What do I have to give up?

Will it make me unpopular?

Will I be uncomfortable?

Will I have to battle my fears?

On and on and on...

I am a job seeker on Godster.com, but there is nothing online for me because I want to actually send myself and get God's approval for the mission. I want to be able to tell everyone "Yes, I became a billionaire in yogurt manufacturing and Starbucks real estate because I felt God calling me to it." Build my own Kingdom and get to put a sign out in front of it claiming God sold it to me.

That is my ultimate game.

The lyrics to my song are honestly "Here am I, Lord, give me what I want right now and send that other guy to do your difficult work."

But that is not where I need to be—I need to change my tune.

I need to take an honest look at my conditions and exceptions and then surrender them to God. Maybe you do, too.

A Closing Exercise: Take a minute to pray. Ask God to show you what exceptions you carry into job interviews with Him and list them below. Get as specific as possible. Write down those things you would not want to be a part of –your narrowing parameters that limit the search results. Then ask God to remove them. He will, and you will soon find yourself doing His Will.

Q & A

—Would you be willing to drop everything and make God's Kingdom your priority? What do you think that means?

—How do you think your cultural upbringing has made it more difficult for you to go anywhere and do anything for God?

—How would you say that you are a spoiled brat?

—Do you ever make excuses for yourself so that you don't have to do something for God?

—Do you think there is an over-emphasis on "doing" for God?

—How should someone balance willingness to do for God with a willingness to seek intimacy with God?

—Do you think there are seasons of "not doing" for God? Seasons where rest and learning take precedence over accomplishing things for Him?

—Have you ever felt judged by others for not being as active/ effective/daring as they are?

—Do you know what part of the Body of Christ that you are? Where do you fit into the Body of Christ? Are there certain roles that come along with your placement? Do you have a definitive calling?

Hale-Bopping

You have probably heard by now about the 39 people who put on Nikes and matching outfits and then killed themselves in hopes of riding on the back of the Hale-Bopp comet. So, I won't bore you with all of the details. But one thing that really blows my mind about the whole event is this: six of the men in the group castrated themselves—voluntarily. That's right. They snipped off their private parts and became Ken dolls and they did it months before their suicides. Why? Because their leader told them to. Incredible, huh? People chopping off important items and then taking their lives because one old dude with wild eyes told them to.

This got me to thinking about other dedicated groups and individuals:

Mormons who take two years out of their lives to do the knock-knock, ties, and bikes tour all over the world because they believe in getting a planet of their own someday.

Suicide bombers who splatter themselves all over Middle Eastern Cafes because they believe in their cause and in their heavens.

Scientologists who either slave away in work camps or pay thousands of dollars to level up because they believe in thetans, Xenu and Tom Cruise.

Marines who get their heads shaved and personalities reduced so that they can be ready to kill an "enemy."

The Jewish people from the Old Testament who, when told of God's new command to be circumcised, allowed the painful knives to set them apart, because they were sure it was important.

This sort of commitment is revealed in one of my favorite movies: *The Karate Kid.* Remember when Mr. Miyagi told Daniel to wax on, wax off? He did it. When he told him to sand the deck, he sanded the deck. When he told him to paint the fence, he painted the fence. Why? All because he had signed up as a student under a man he trusted to teach him karate.

Take a look at all of these people. All of them are volunteers. All of them have a leader whom they trust without negotiation. All of them have beliefs and codes, which guide them and from which they do not deviate. And all of them are willing to sacrifice everything.

Now to my big questions: What about us Christians? Didn't we volunteer to be made into disciples? Haven't we bowed down to a leader and called Him our Lord? Don't we have beliefs and codes that we should be radically obeying? Are we not called to an obedience that requires sacrifice and struggle?

On paper, we are the same in our dedication. But in reality, I have to say that we suck at all of the above. We said yes to discipleship, but we refuse to lay down the necessary things to become disciples. We said yes to Jesus, but only allow Him to be Lord, when we agree or when we feel comfortable with it. We have beliefs, but they do not determine the way we live. We accept the call to obey, but we are not committed to actualizing it.

I have come to the conclusion that as a whole, we are not dedicated people. We are not really that committed. We do not knock on doors. We do not take time out of our schedules. We do not lay down our lives. We do not slave away at anything. We refuse to slice away anything that might cause us pain or loss. We complain and we negotiate and we disrespect our Master.

And I have to wonder why...

I have to ask: Why is my commitment level such that I will go to the edges of my comfort zone for Jesus, but no further? (I'm going to be honest—if the wax-on causes me to have a blister, I am going to tell the Messiah to wax-off.)

Why is our commitment level such that we struggle when asked to witness, to pray, to study, to do justice, or even to just give away our money?

Do we need Jesus to be more like a drill sergeant? Do we need the Holy Spirit to stand in front of us and call us maggots and demand that we give him 100 pushups every time we think of falling short?

I don't think so.

But I do wonder if it might help for the church and its leadership to set the bar a bit higher for its people. Where are the expectations for the Christians? Why aren't they being communicated with from day one? Why aren't there immediate consequences dished out to those who refuse to live by them? I think we have lived in fear of our congregations' rejection. We do not want them to leave us behind and so we do all the fence painting for them. We protect them from the costs of Christianity and pay their bills for them with a grace that is false. And as a result, we are a people without dedication. Try bringing a word as difficult as circumcision today and watch your crowds relocate. To tell you the truth, I would be fine with that. Less would probably be more. Get rid of the lazy karate students. Throw them in the brig. Just give me the few and the proud.

Side note: You will lose people if you call on them to live out a dedicated Christianity. If you set Biblical expectations like Jesus did, you will probably also be rejected. The good news just keeps on coming...

Q & A

—How do you think people would describe your walk with God?

—Are you willing to be a Jesus Fanatic (AKA regular disciple of Jesus)? What would that even look like in your life at home, at work, in relationships, etc.?

—Do you think that God really wants such outward displays of "commitment" from His people? What are some good biblical arguments for both sides?

—How do fear, culture, personality, external perceptions, and busyness play parts in limiting your full-on dedication to God's forceful movements on this planet?

—Read Hebrews 11:32-39 and discuss why you think these people did what they did?

—How should we think about this dedication without guilt?

Time Spent

In my adult life—age 18 to age 40—22 years—I have had the opportunity to live for approximately 8030 days. In those days, I have been awake for approximately 128,480 hours. How have I spent those hours? It is interesting to check. It might tell me what my life priorities have been up to this moment and allow me to live better in the future.

So here are my best guesses:

I have seen about 750 movies at an average of 2 hours each. That's 1,500 hours on movies.

I have watched about 2 hours of TV a day, which equals about 16,060 hours for television.

I have read about thirty minutes a day or about 3,100 hours total.

I have worked about 2,000 hours per year, which puts me at 44,000 hours.

I have spent 10,000 hours on the Internet.

I have played about 5,000 hours of board games, cards, or sports.

I have spent about 4,500 hours driving from place to place.

I have spent about 8,000 hours studying the Bible and praying and another 3,000 hours doing ministry.

I have spent approximately 15,000 hours eating, 8,200 hours on getting ready for the day, 7,200 hours talking on the telephone. And the rest of my time has probably been spent on a mix of bathroom use, sinning, waiting in lines, shopping, and exercising.

What does this little list tell me? The main thing that stands out is this: Movies plus Television plus Reading plus Internet plus Games equals about 35,000 hours of my life which have been spent on entertainment and diversion. That is over one half of my life which has been given to Hollywood and Sports Center and Tabloid magazines and poker and email.

More than 25% of my life traded in for very little return.

Yes, I have experienced the wonders of Seinfeld, soaked in the bright lights of about 50 great films, kept up with celebrity lives, and surfed on the best and the worst of the World Wide Web. But where has it gotten me? Did God put me on this planet and say: "Go, sleep, eat, play and be entertained"? Because if He didn't, I don't think I'm going to be hearing the "Well Done, Good and Faithful Servant" speech when I arrive at the Heavenly gates.

Sure, I might be able to take out Peter and John the Baptist in Texas Hold 'em or Risk and I will probably be able to stump the Holy Spirit on Super Bowl stats and I bet that my well-crafted Top-30 movie list and nicely built iTunes account will impress Noah, who most certainly would have liked an iPod and an HD theatre system on the Ark.

But this is not a life well lived—just one tenth of it on seeking God and doing His will is barely a tithe of time. It is like giving someone a million bucks and watching him waste $250,000 on Pokemon cards and accessories.

Now, I have to ask the question: Why do I live this way? Is this lifestyle a conformity to culture and a bondage to technology diversion? Is there a way to break out of this sort of life?

I justify it every day. Everyday, I justify it. I am on a treadmill. I'm in a videogame and watching Pac-Man devour my dots.

I'll bet if I would trade my diversions—at least some of them—to help others around me, the world would be a better place.

But I'll also bet that I don't do the trade. What a deeply disappointing realization. I live for my stomach, my sleep, Facebook and Twitter, and fun and games. I expect to get only a few rewards in Heaven for a life lived like this. I am an American Idol tryout worse than William Hung.

If Jesus had not come, I'd surely be burned to a crisp. Some things need to change.

Q & A

—How would you describe the way you spend time?

—When you hear the words "Time Management," what do you think of specifically?

—Do you think God wants time to be managed well or fully maximized, and what would that mean to you?

—What time wasters do you engage in? What time wasters are you willing to let go?

—Do you handle your time like it is a valuable resource and use it for eternal things? What examples would you give of this?

—What do you think would help you use time in ways that would please God?

—If you knew exactly how much time you had on this earth, how would it affect the way you spend that time?

Last Day

If someone said to me that this was my last day on earth, I would smile.

Why?

Because I have straight teeth.

And if it happened to be Friday, I would smile bigger because that would mean I have *Killer Pawn Shop Storage War Battlefields* on DVR, and I would get to spend my last breaths watching quality television.

Seriously, I need to live better.

This might be my last day, and what a shame it would be if I kept on wasting time on crappy TV and sports magazines and avoided emails.

What are people going to say about me at my funeral?

I was odd.

I was very aware of Dallas Cowboy statistics.

I had a way with picking good grocery store fruit.

I looked in the mirror a lot.

I worked hard twice a week.

I blogged meaningless ploddings of brain matter.

I wrote unread books.

I constantly promised to seek God more.

I constantly broke my promises.

I cleared Nintendo Super Mario Brothers without losing a man.

I won prom king.

I had interesting taste in movies.

I lost touch with friends.

I got several degrees.

I took so much for granted.

I had a wiener dog named Adolph that I really did not feed very often.

I once taught English in China.

I missed a million opportunities to talk to people about Jesus.

I started lots of great projects that I could not finish.

I had a pretty good golf drive.

I dominated in Risk.

I once did a mission in Kazakhstan.

I was a pusher in tennis.

I was sarcastic and fairly amusing.

I had hemorrhoids.

I did a bit of good for people around me.

I loved my family.

And that is fine, but does all that make for a great life?

And is it worth even buying a nice casket for?

Wow—do I ever need to shape up!

I know the good I ought to do—but I do not do enough of it.

Who will volunteer to shake me out of the sleepy hollow?

Q & A

—What sort of alarm clocks has God set for you to wake you up to a better version of living? Are you hitting snooze?

—How have you put your "accomplishments" under the quality-of-life microscope to see how they really look in light of the truly important things?

—Do you ever work hard to do things that at the time seem super important, but upon future reflection seem as silly as putty?

—How do you let people and organizations around you elevate tasks to a status of vital/crucial?

—What happens when you realize that most things you engage in are not that important?

—In other words, when you start to see through the supposedly "important things" and recognize them for what they really are, how do you go ahead and do *what must be done* with a good attitude?

The Knew and Do?

Solomon choked.

The son of David and Bathsheba became king and was given more wisdom than anyone on Earth.

And he used it to make so many wise decisions for others. And he wrote some cool proverbs. And Ecclesiastes rocks.

But when it came to his own life, he blew it.

Here is something that we should never ever forget: Solomon knew better, but he did not do better.

Check out I Kings 1. It is an astounding account of the wisest man on the planet knowing what God wanted him to do and what not to do.

"Don't intermarry with the women of other nations because they will turn your heart from me."

But Solomon did it anyway. He married lots of women from other nations. And these women turned his heart from the Lord and got him to worship their sucky, fake gods.

Solomon the Wise acting a fool. Sometimes when I read this chapter I cannot believe what I am seeing: a man who had followed God wholeheartedly, the man who built God's temple, who grew up under his father David and must have learned a thing or two about not screwing his life up with a woman. Solomon let his heart dictate his actions. His heart held fast to the ladies. They became more important to him than honoring the One who had made him a rich man and a stud.

Was it sexual addiction? Maybe.

Was he the Hugh Hefner of his day? I think so—he had a harem and hundreds of mattress partners. (He would have been a Reality Show for sure.)

Terrible.

Wholehearted to part-hearted.

He got some and then he got some more. And then he started building temples and worship sites for their gods. And their gods became his gods. And God got really pissed off at him and promised to take away his kingdom—which He did in the following generation.

Solomon knew better. But he did not do better.

Does that sound familiar to you?

It does to me.

I am not near as wise as Solomon, but I know enough. And my knowledge of what God wants from me should drive me onto straight paths. Yet while I know better, I do not always do better. In fact, on most days, I choose to follow a heart's cry that screams for worldly things—a heart's cry that insists on getting approval from people—a heart's tantrum that kicks and screams and kicks the crap out of the grace Jesus came to give me.

I pre-meditate making mistakes. I lead myself into the wilderness and easily locate comfort. I mis-aim on purpose—arrows flying left and right.

And why?

Do I want to anger God?

It is rare that I consider how to please God. It is common instead that I push God's buttons—almost taunt Him with my foolish choices that overcome a wise mind.

Sure, God is slow to anger. But just because He is slow does not mean He won't get there eventually—especially if I am putting my foot on his foot that pounds down on the accelerator.

Do you feel the push?

Are you like me?

Can we help each other slow this pattern down?

Can we become fools who do the words of Jesus rather than the preachers who do the sermon's opposite?

Can we know better and do better?

I need to sit down and ask God today: What have I given my heart to? Who or what makes me build temples for them over God? Can I have an extra ladle of grace to keep me near You?

Q & A

—What parts of this world threaten to capture your heart and lead you away from God? What does your heart hold fast to?

—When have you known better, but not done better? Would you say that this is a common thing for you?

—How does the Holy Spirit distribute supernatural wisdom to you?

—Discuss times when you've found yourself doing sinful life junk that you truly thought you weren't even capable of doing. In other words, when have you entered the places of "Shock and Awe" screw-ups?

—Why do you think Solomon gave himself over to those types of screw-ups when he knew that God was the best option? When he knew the consequences of his actions?

—Does this chapter help you realize something about the difference between having wisdom and applying wisdom?

Forget You, Too

The first chapter of Ecclesiastes says that we will most likely not be remembered very long past our deaths. This is true. After the obituaries and the memorials and a couple of generations, the memory of (most of) us fades to black.

Who will know Ben Donley fifty years after his passing? Who will give a crap that I shot golf in the low 80's, played solid ping-pong, wore fedoras, and wrote books very few humans read (though I am big in Tibet)? Who will be able to see my bald spot on the television and identify me as the man who can control minds and create cloud movements? Who will search out my headstone (made of indestructible lettuce) and place appropriate warrior badges there?

Not many.

Who will know you?

This leads me to a few thought processes:

Since we are so quick to be forgotten, why do we worry so much about how others perceive us in the present? I am telling you, you've got some freedom for the future. You could poop in your pants today or projectile vomit in public spaces tomorrow and over time, people will forget—maybe even before you die—unless you do these things at consecutive weddings and funerals.

Anyway, we live so carefully. We prep our faces and our morning masks and our appropriate responses and polite reactions so we do not make a bad impression on other humans, and we find they do the same for us. We want so badly for people to recall us as normal good citizens who are good at many things and bad at few. Waste of time.

This fact also makes we wonder why we try so hard to achieve and accomplish so much. To become someone is important only to a few, and those few will take your amazing inventions and words to the grave with them. Most of what you do to be remembered is lost right about when you retire. Like getting the high score in Galaga and putting your initials in—just pull the plug on the game and you are gone.

This fact also makes me think of how cool it is that God remembers each of us by name. Whether normal, simple, heroic, disgusting, alive, dead, or just plagued by "dream hair," God sees you now as wonderful and will not have to look at Facebook to recall who you are when you drop dead and end up before Him. God knows my baldness. He knows my bests and my worsts from the time I began, and He will treasure me through generations called the eternal.

Screw the world and its attempt to make me seize its day. Carpe Diem is dead. Carpe Heaven. Carpe Kingdom. If I want to be remembered by the only One who never forgets, I must live with the reminder that those around me must get less attention than Jesus. I must decrease. God must increase. The world must disappear.

PS. If I do pass away earlier than expected, would any of you be kind enough to come by my gravesite and put some ranch dressing on the headstone once in a while? I'd appreciate it...

Q & A

—How does the reality of not being remembered long after your death affect you?

—How does this reality change the way you set goals or plan your accomplishments?

—How does the world try to counter this truth? What does it try to tell us about how to live? About how to be memorable?

—Do you ever put pressure on yourself to be memorable? How have you attempted to leave your mark on this planet?

—Is it hard for you to accept the fact that you are easily forgotten? Easily replaceable? Not invaluable?

—How does this truth affect you in a positive way?

—How can you spend more time and energy doing that which will be remembered in the eternal?

—What is memorable to God?

—How does it make you feel when you consider that God remembers you and considers you eternally valuable?

Interfaith Discussions

Check out 2 Kings 23. I don't think anyone has to wonder how Josiah of the Old Testament would have felt about Interfaith Discussions.

Question: Anyone out there want to try out this sort of Josiah-Reformation? I don't even have the guts to applaud Josiah from thousands of years later. Why? I have been through tolerance training so I am always extra-nice to my fellow religions. Even if they are frighteningly wrong and are teaching things that will ultimately destroy people's souls, I restrain myself. I am polite. I have etiquette. And I am happy to see you do as well. (Last statement said with my pinky finger sticking out daintily and a salad fork in hand.)

Interfaith Discussions—Those meetings between Protestant pastors, Jewish Rabbis, Buddhist monks, Muslim imams, Hindu priests and every other Kabbalic Madonna or Scientological personality test proctor on the planet—Those sacred gatherings held on neutral fields in Five-Star Conference rooms—Voices from every angle claiming wisdom about cultural issues—Extra-tolerant humans dressed in various clothing walking on egg shells and avoiding any sort of exclusive 'my way or the hellway' sort of talk. Just Aretha Franklin-style R-E-S-P-E-C-T for all religions. Handshakes and winky nods of appreciation for shared vocation. Held hands and prayers sent up to God or god or blod or Barney the dinosaur. Words written down and proclaimed to nothing and to no one in particular. The kind of prayers that go straight to the voicemail of a defunct dot.com in the sky. (Seriously, which deity wants to pick up that phone call? It would just be a telemarketing voice at the other end that doesn't know with whom it wants to speak.)

What a waste!!!

Christians need to stop being so polite. The Muslims are feared. We are just worship-gathering wienies who want to harmonize with the enemies of God. It seems we are just money-loving "occupiers" who sit and whine but don't throw stones.

How many Baal prophets did Elijah smoke in one day?

Pass out the machetes, not the palm branches.

Forget the sermon for a year and fight with the warriors.

For once, I'd like to leave church with blood on my face.

Q & A

—Why do you think we hand ourselves over to these useless sessions?

—Why do God's people believe that it is important to be tolerant when our Bible makes it very clear that intolerance is a key factor in being a true follower of Jesus?

—What is your definition of intolerance? What is the actual definition of intolerance?

—Do you think that Western Christians have gotten swept up in an inclusion movement that frustrates God?

—Do you believe that if God does not tolerate it, you should not tolerate it? Or do you tend to apologize for how direct the Bible can be about this behavior?

—Do you care more about what people think about you than what God thinks? How have these people pleasing and culture pleasing tendencies shown up in your life?

Damn

Famous sermon: Some preacher somewhere stood up and made three simple statements, which shook his congregation:

1. Thirty million men, women and children will starve to death today.

2. Most people do not give a damn.

3. Even worse, most of you are more concerned about my saying the word "damn" than the fact that 30 million people are unnecessarily dying daily.

This brings up an important question for every Christian everywhere: do you give a damn? Not just about the 30 million starvers, but about anyone who is struggling, or about anything meaningful? I ask because I suffer from a tendency to care about the wrong things. I cringe and squirm and yell at my TV when Tony Romo drops a snap for the Dallas Cowboys. I have hours of passionate conversation about the injustices of Academy Award nominees. In Christian circles, I tend to care a lot about moral issues and some useless theological arguments. But I don't really give much thought or have any passionate concern for women trapped by sex traffickers, civilians blown up by accidental bombs, or homeless kids walking around with their shopping cart parents.

I hate this about myself—this misplaced concern—this culture-trained heart for sports, tabloid and sitcom characters—this "who gives a damn" attitude.

Mother Teresa frowns down at me. I could not show you Calcutta on a map.

I am a follower of Jesus. I should know better. I should feel more. But I don't. And I am not alone, am I? I have a nervous feeling that I'm in the Western Christian majority—one of the many arrogant, overfed, and unconcerned 'disciples' of Jesus Christ who don't do much to live up to the role or title—morally careful people who care about worship style and pew comfort, but who could care less about the conditions of the needy, the broken, and the hungry. I'm the king of these fools. But I have been in my Bible like crazy lately and it's time that I emulate someone who did care: Nehemiah.

I want to be more like Nehemiah. Why?

When Nehemiah heard his people were struggling, he took it to heart, he dropped to his face, he cried out for mercy, then he risked his security and comfortable position and actually did something about it. He gathered supplies, checked out the misery for himself, unified a divided community, battled intimidating enemies, and built a wall that saved Israel and brought them back to life. In less than six months, a regular man with the right amount of concern that was aimed at something important transformed an entire nation.

Now I am not looking to change the Sudan in six months. I am not Bono. But I'd sure better change my heart and start giving a damn. Even if that "damn" leads me to do something as small as taking one life and helping to build it back up—a prostitute or a homeless guy or a kid who needs to know that he is worth something. Just let me care about someone or something that matters. And may this concern of mine be big enough to bring me to my knees in tears. And may this concern of mine be big enough to take me out of my regular scheduled programming. And may this concern of mine for CNN be exchanged once and for all so that walls get built and people get helped.

Do you want to join me?

Okay. Skip a Super Bowl party and cancel your subscription to *Forbes* and dump the idea that your lives are the bottom line. Then get ready to move.

Here are a few steps:

-Look around—that's right. Pay attention to the world around you. Don't duck your head when you see a guy with a "help me" sign. Don't change the channel when the skinny black kids come into view. Don't just read the sports or entertainment page. Find out what is going on in this world that needs a problem solver. Then make a list of what you find.

-Make these problems your problem—If my computer does not work, I will work through the night finding the solution so that I can be connected to the Web and my documents. The computer is my problem and I do whatever I can to solve it as soon as I can. I need to take the same attitude in life. I don't just need to shake my noggin side to side and say something compassionate. The world's problems are my problems and I need to take responsibility. The single mom's problems are my problems, and I'd better do something to help out. The education system has crashed, and I'd better get involved.

-Act first in prayer—Get on your face and ask God for justice, mercy, and wisdom as how to best serve the situation. Pray hard about whatever it is—make it a part of your regular intercession time. Make it as important as your own forgiveness and blessing requests. Tell God that you are at least a portion as concerned as He is and sign up for His recovery project.

-Follow it all the way through—Enough of the old college tries. We need to be Good Samaritans about this. Use our time, energy, and money to guarantee that full healing occurs. Do what we can now and do everything we can later. Just as Nehemiah wasn't satisfied with a half-built wall, we shouldn't be either.

-Form a team—Nehemiah did not do it alone and with millions of Christians at your disposal, you will not have to either. Recruit a group of problem solvers and get out there to deal with the millions of individuals and community messes which have been made.

I am sure there is much more, but this is all I will say here. Except a reminder to give a damn everyday for the rest of your days— God will bless that move.

Q & A

—What if the preacher had said "fuck" instead of "damn?" Would you have been shocked and offended by his use of that word? How long do you think it would have been before that preacher was fired?

—What do you think would actually stir a group of indifferent Christians into action for a global cause? For a local cause?

—What has de-sensitized you to the problems crushing people around the world?

—Where would you say that you fall on the continuum between indifferent and actively engaged?

—What keeps you from getting involved with helping others?

—Do you actively seek solitude and intimacy with God so that you can be filled with His Spirit and thus empowered to tackle situations/issues much larger than you can handle?

Emergent Church?

Zeitgeists, meta-narratives, glockenspiels, Kierkegaards, quantum spiritualities, post-post-modernistic cohortic journeys, neo-orthodoxical house churches, art history prayer stations, monastic jogathons, relevant and relative-mystic social justice conversations, missional 4.5 minute un-sermons and mass graves for the conservatives who still believe in a literal, eternal Hell.

"Check us out, world. We are the ultra-intellectual Christians, and we are more clever than ever. Don't accuse us of being our parents. Accuse us of being our great-great-great-great grandparents who once hung with Jesuits and St. Francis at the Ivy League monk bar.

We are Generation A. But with blogs and brains and Billabongs."

I'm not trying to be mean.

But come on, people. I went to a couple of your conferences and felt like I was at the Tower of Babel after-party. What is with the lingo? Do I have to pay extra for a translator? Seriously, how many big words can you use? How many abstract philosophies can you reference? Can't someone just read the NIV version of the Beatitudes without mentioning Tolstoy?

Listen, I understand the temptation to appear hip and educated. I know insecurity, and I want to stand out, too. I, like you, have also shoved a ton of University Humanities Department information into my mind and need somewhere to dump it. I too am a cleverness addict with knowledge of the dialectic, a self-published book about *The Matrix*, and several sermon files dedicated to linking the lost gospels to Radiohead's discography.

But let's not be too high-minded. Let's not forget that we are dumb sheep and that we believe in some pretty strange stuff. Demons and Ghosts and Resurrections. These are things that you cannot hide behind a Harvard degree or well-crafted Nietzsche simile.

Let's also remember that God will frustrate the intelligence of the intelligent. Keep changing the rules and getting more tolerant of shit that God says is abominable, and I'm going to come at you, too. With my love and a flamethrower, because love wins. (Uhhhh. Yeah, love for God and His orthodox truth wins.)

So let's stop the emerging and submerge instead. Go deep in God, put the academic journals down, and exegete some Flintstones.

Q & A

—What do you think about the Emergent Church movement?

—What do you think are the most positive things about what the Emergents are trying to do?

—What do you think are the most disturbing things about what the Emergents are trying to accomplish?

—Why do think that more and more people are challenging and/or resisting the following Orthodox stances: Unrepentant and rebellious people go to Hell, Jesus is the only way to Heaven, and Lordship is a necessary part of the Christian covenant?

—How do you respond to those who insist that the rules can and should be changed?

—What do you think the words of Jesus to the Seven Churches in Revelation have to say about God and His will for the Body?

Clearing Something Up

I just want to toss something out there into the great wide open of Christian discussion. I'm sure it has been said by millions of others already and that I have just not been privy to the conversations. But just in case it has not been mentioned outside of the Aramaic Journals and Emergent Church canons, I want to go ahead and clear something up for the masses that tend to drive me crazy with their dumb ideas about God.

Here's the deal: Jesus is eternal. He did not come into existence in the manger. He was right there with the Father and the Holy Spirit since the very beginning. Do you understand what this means?

It means that all the times God the Father passed down laws that a lot of people hated, Jesus and the Holy Spirit were there in full agreement with Him. Thumbs up.

It also means that when The Father said that certain behaviors were sins that were deserving of death and Hell, Jesus and the Holy Spirit were in agreement. They knew what was what and they were on board.

So hear this loud and clear: Jesus was not the bleeding heart dissenting vote against the angry, mean, Old Testament Father's woes and judgments. He was totally cool with them. He completely agreed.

So when you start talking about agreeing or disagreeing with what the Father God of the Old Testament put into play as far as laws and woes, you are also talking about what the Holy Spirit and what Mr. Loving Jesus the Savior thought were perfect rulings. You cannot separate eternal Jesus with manger/Earth Jesus when it comes to His ideas, rules, laws, beliefs, and set-ups.

So, we need to stop re-writing what the Father, Son, and Holy Spirit never changed. It's easy to gain groupies and adoring crowds if you allow everyone off the hook Gaga-style. But, to change God's rules is dangerous. And to get others to change their behaviors and their beliefs because of these rule changes is just not "loving."

And for you Gentiles out there who want to keep fighting for your rights to be a deviant and justify it as a birthright, please read Acts 15 over and over until you realize that the Holy Spirit gave clear instructions to all of us non-Jews which can be stated as clearly as this: The sexual laws in the Levitical code still apply to us. We may not have all of the sacrificial requirements to complete, and we don't have any circumcision to handle, but the sexual code must still be followed.

This all should make perfect sense. If it doesn't, read your Bible more. You have the Law and the Prophets and it's best to know them and apply them now before a chasm gets too big to cross.

Q & A

—Why do you think that Christians do not read their whole Bible?

—What percentage of people in the U.S. would you guess have actually studied the entire Word and filter life and interpretations through humble prayer?

—Why don't more churches teach the entire Bible rather than hitting the pop topics and verses again and again?

—What do you think might motivate people to read and study their whole Bibles?

—Do you understand that despite covenantal shifts that God makes with various groups of people, God does not change?

—Why is Acts 15 such a significant chapter for Gentiles living today under the New Covenant? How does it connect us to and disconnect us from the Mosaic Laws?

Truth Hurts

One thing I have learned: people do not appreciate truth *if* it goes against them.

Truth, when it matches up with someone's current beliefs and decisions, is applauded like the President at the State of the Union. But truth that delivers a blow to the mindset that is bubble-bathing in deception gets crucified. And don't be fooled. It does not matter who delivers such truth. No one, no matter how great they are, no matter how beloved they are, can deliver this sort of truth and live long. Especially if a majority group stakes its foundation or profit on the opposite.

I could give many examples, but the one most fascinating to me is the one that features Jesus very early in his ministry. Check it out with me in Luke 4:14-30.

In these verses, Jesus is a miracle-working crowd favorite. But then he tells his Jewish crowd that God is open to outsiders. He tells them that their own wonderful prophets, Elijah and Elisha, were sent to bless foreigners (the widow and Naaman) over and against them. Jesus smacks their pride. He confronts their long-held belief that Israel is the only nation that God cares for. And what happens? Jesus is immediately hated. Hated so much that the crucifixion almost becomes unnecessary. This crowd, who just got dealt some important truth, takes Jesus—the recently loved Jesus—to the edge of a cliff to throw him off.

You see, this crowd just heard truth that did not agree with them and this crowd decided to murder the messenger—Savior or no Savior.

My first thought after reflecting on this is how often I take Jesus to the cliff when he opens his big mouth to utter truth that hurts me. I am surprised that he doesn't greet me in prayer with a parachute on his back.

No wonder preachers and politicians deal out the happy-happy-joy-joy truths rather than honest declarations of God's word. The Minor Prophets and the Woe sermons do not warm the crowd like Psalm 23 does.

Some advice to you pastors out there:

1. Always begin your painful speeches with several good jokes before you punch people in the head with the word of God. As Mary Poppins sang, "A spoonful of sugar helps the medicine go down."

2. Make sure that you are not anywhere near a cliff or even a tall stage.

Seriously, the people of God are not much different now than they were in Jesus's day. The people of God still want to hear sermons that sit right in their minds and stomachs. And if you hand out the harsh truths, which riddle the pages of the Old and New Testaments, you can pretty much guarantee either an angry attendance that will soon toss out your convicting voice or an exiting audience that will leave you behind and find some other church that has some kinder, gentler voice that can soothe their tired souls.

Tickle-Me Pastors are the Christmastime rage every year and the prophets always get burned.

Q & A

—Have you ever had truth hurt you?

—When have you responded correctly to hard truth? When have you responded badly to hard truth?

—How do you react to truth that calls you to change your course or your behavior? How do you treat people who are bold enough to be your truth tellers?

—What is the best way to speak truth to people? What does it look like in the real world?

—How open are you to correction? Do you invite constructive criticism or avoid it at all costs?

Jack and Diane

"Oh yeah, life goes on. Long after the thrill of living is gone."

Jack and Diane and John Cougar and you and me.

If you have enough life experience, you know these words to be true. When your eyes get opened and you've tried all the diversions, tasted some of the drugs, watched enough television and movies, seen your favorite bands live, traveled into new locales, and basically filled your senses with all that this world has to offer, you realize that life is not that exciting—not that thrilling. Yes, there are the rushes of sex and ambition and conquest and winning and jumping out of airplanes, but each of them carry short-lived highs and create all sorts of headaches and hangovers.

Every day beyond that realization is a Bigfoot step to the edge of an existential skyscraper ledge, which has a sickening beyond. Once you've seen the void of your pursuits and once the thrill has been smoothed down, you recognize that you have done it "all" and that the "all" was empty. You feel cheated and are left with a few options: Kill yourself, get higher and higher, get fatter and fatter, get richer and richer, get smarter and smarter, have more kids, wish for the glory days when the thrill still thrilled, or shop 'til you drop at the Wal-Marts and shopping malls of this world until the sand runs out. You might join a cause and save some animals. You might set up an insightful blog. You might backpack in Europe. You might get your name put on a building. You might discover the cure to a disease. You might throw your hands up and become a homeless dropout. It does not matter. They are all equally meaningless.

The only thing that matters is seeking God—knowing Him and being known—being emptied and being filled.

Cool clubs do not matter. Fine food does not matter. Golf scores do not matter. Your favorite team's making it to the playoffs doesn't matter. Sleeping with your Cinderella or Prince Charming doesn't matter. Getting straight A's doesn't matter. Having a seven-figure salary doesn't matter. Looking good at age 65 doesn't matter. Running a marathon doesn't matter. Making a business more profitable doesn't matter. Your child getting into Yale doesn't matter. Writing a bestseller doesn't matter. Owning a nice house doesn't matter. Being a great family doesn't matter.

You name it. It does not mean a thing.

Even if everyone else says that it does. Even if it makes you feel worth. Still it doesn't mean a thing. And you can deny it all you want and act like the ledge on that skyscraper doesn't exist, but you know down deep in your bones that it does. You feel it. The thrill is going, going, gone. The world has been a liar all your life—a false advertisement and you are still walking around in its T-shirt as a franchise rep for the folly. And I imagine that the only reason you continue to do it is because you've been too busy to change or too scared to seek another option or too much of a conformist to be different than the rest.

Well, here and now is a phone call from God's right hand to you— from the place where real joy and pleasure and thrill reside. It's ringing on your tiny little cell phone and if you screen the call, I say that you deserve the wasted life of Jack and Diane. No skin off of me if you don't answer. I do not get rewarded if you choose to stay or to go. Still, I work for the company's call center and I am screaming at you: Stop chasing the wind. Let God blow you away.

Q & A

—Have you hit the point in life when the thrill has gone?

—What would you say is the typical human response to the reality of life's boredom?

—Are you a thrill seeker? In what ways?

—Do you ever expect God to give you a thrilling spiritual feeling? Does He owe you that?

—Do you ever get the feeling that the worst part of Jesus's time on Earth was the 32.9 years he had to hang out pre-crucifixion?

—How does technology try to keep us thrilled? How is it doing that with you?

—How are we supposed to "feel" about the world anyway? Are you groaning with the rest of creation as you await the new creation? Or are you trying to suck out some useless juice from the old one?

Your Will Be Done???

Isaiah 53:10—Yet it was the LORD's will to crush him and cause him to suffer.

This prophetic chapter in Isaiah tells us that the Messiah was not to be attractive. The Messiah would be pushed aside, pushed around, and punished.

Punished.

It clearly states that it was God's will to crush him and cause him to suffer.

"What?"

God's will to crush a person whom He loves?

That is about forty miles outside of the box.

But sometimes God's will is to crush someone—to put his own finger—no make that His brass knuckles—on top of someone and press down until blood spills out—until life is gone—until everything changes.

When I pray for God's will to be done, I rarely think that God's Will might include my suffering—my crushing—my death.

Me: "God, Your will be done—unless it hurts me..."

Jesus: "Father, Your will be done—even as it hurts me..."

Big difference there.

We should not be disappointed when His will is done and it undoes us as men and women. His will is good and pleasing and perfect, but that does not mean His will feels good.

Last year, as God pressed down hard on me, leaving me wanting to die—not just for a second or two, but every moment of every day for too many days to count, I despised this fact that God can destroy someone He loves.

And my understanding of it was that it was Him doing it to me. And His reason for doing this to me: to help me let go of control, to show me that I had been hating myself since age five, to lead me past the pain of the cross and into the joy that can come only after the self dies and the Spirit lives, to teach me to love me even at my worst, to let me know that it is better than okay to be unimpressive and unsuccessful.

I hesitate these days when I ask for God's will, but I go ahead and say it—last time I did it, He dragged me through the darkest places and the muddiest, bloodiest, cruelest internal crap. And I hated everyone around me. And I hated that I could not stop crying . And I hated how weak I was, how weak I was showing myself to everyone around me. What a disappointment. What a failure. I wished that my arm He was using to pull me forward would just tear off at some magical shoulder perforations and that He would leave me there.

The footprints of God on my beach had been erased by my body being pulled behind Him.

My body left a narrow path and I still recall every second of the pain and pressure. I wondered if I would have a wife after it—I wondered if I would have a job after it—I wondered if I would have a mind after it.

I wondered and then I stopped wondering. I found myself too tired to wonder

I assumed I was going to die or get put into a psych ward.

Nothing tasted good. Nothing sounded interesting. Bed and covers and fetal position were my only comforts.

But it has been 5 months since His will shifted, and I have shifted.

But I am not the same man I was.

I could never be the same man I was.

And I will not speak the same way or counsel the same way.

I now have something to say if He wants me to. If not, I will live a simple, quiet life.

A thankful life.

A life that was seemingly great until it ran into God's will.

A life that was actually spoiled rotten until it ran into God's will.

A life that is now quite weird and funny and cherished.

A life that required a prostrate man dripping bloody tears and begging for an end to the drag.

May we all be thankful.

May we all keep saying loud and clear: "Your will be done," no matter what that might mean.

Q & A

—What do you truly expect when you pray for God's will to be done in your life?

—Do you ask for God's will to extend into all areas of your life? Are you cool if His will means that you experience loss or trouble?

—When you ask for God's will to be done, are you also completely willing to accept whatever that brings?

—In what areas of life would you have the hardest time handling God's will if it happened to bring struggle?

—How do you think your will and God's will compare and contrast in various areas of your life?

—Do you ever fight with God about when things do not go as you thought they might? How does that usually go?

—What do you think about adopting a full-on attitude of acceptance with God rather than mixing it all together with human expectation? How might acceptance of whatever God wants change the way you go about life?

Videotape

At the end of every day, if I was shown a videotape of my recent behavior, how I related to people, how I treated my family, how I spoke to my wife, how I frowned more than I smiled, how I used my time, how I served my self, how I ignored others, how I missed opportunity after opportunity, I imagine that I would be shocked and I imagine I would change.

I wish that I had the chance to review my life as I went. Am I doing well? I don't know.

I can't help but wonder if I am making all sorts of mistakes that I am not aware of. I can't help but wonder if I am doing things to hurt people's feelings. I can't help but wonder if I am saying things that bring people pain.

But there is no videotape.

And without the dailies, I am not so sure what sort of movie my life is going to be.

Will I be *Dumb and Dumber*?

Will I be *Braveheart*?

Or *Rocky 5*?

Q & A

—What movie would you say your life resembles?

—In which genre do you think your life movie would land with Netflix?

—Would you be a likeable character if you were to see your life play out on screen? Or would you be the annoying person that no one in the audience can stand?

—What would be the song playing at the credits of your life so far?

—How do you think you would change your ways if you were able to review your daily tapes?

—Who is the perfect actor to play you? Who would be the obvious choice to direct?

The Eagle Has Landed

Jesus said that he came to give us full lives. Abundant lives. Overflowing lives.

Spacious and prosperous lives.

Lives that lift us off the ground and send us to the upper reaches of the heavens.

Up.

Soaring like eagles. Sounds good to me.

So how is it that we are so "grounded?" So scavenging? So trapped? Sliding along small hallways that close in on us like a *Star Wars* trash compactor? Stuck and complaining? Discouraged and hopeless? Dreading and dreadful? Depressed and medicated?

Soaring eagles?

Not even close. Most of us have not flapped in years.

Instead, most of us have become eagles lining up inside a Foot Locker store buying high-tops and cross-trainers with built-in orthotics, convinced by our enemy that we are meant to walk around rather than fly.

That's right. Our killing, stealing, and destroying enemy has loaded arm weights onto our collective wings and persuaded us to keep our heads down and our shoes laced up for the cruel trudge of survival.

Satan—such a shoe salesman, such a liar, such a thief. How does he do it?

He talks.

He wakes you in the morning with hypnotic, heavy words when you are too tired to resist him. By the time he has finished talking, he has shoved a straw into your heart and slurped away any hope you may have had. It is DRAINAGE. Satan drinks your milkshake.

What is his speech?

He says: don't even bother getting up—today is not going to be good. It is going to be a grind. There is nothing exciting awaiting you, not even in your email—just fake World Cup money give-aways. Not even on TV—it is terrible sit-com night. Today will be the same old food, same old people, same old plans, same old places, same old eight-year old Target clothes in your closet, same old websites, same old meetings, same old you...

And you really cannot disagree with him. It *is* terrible sit-com night, Ramen Noodle boxes do line your cabinets, and Pinterest hasn't lived up to its hype. So what he is saying is pretty accurate. He is not lying. He is just interpreting. Suddenly, you don't want this day at all.

Then he moves to the next thing. He reminds you of how badly you failed the day before—of how you yelled at your spouse or your kid for no good reason—of how you kicked the chihuahua for chewing up the remote control—of how you made a shambles of the entire Sermon on the Mount in just two hours' time. And then he names you "Failure" and "Sinner." And again you have a hard time disagreeing.

Then he reminds you of all the things you left undone from the day before. He shows you how you wasted time on Fox News and the newest *Angry Birds* and *Friends* reruns and *FIFA 2016*. He floats that to-do list of yours in front of your face and shows you that it still exists. And then he names you "Procrastinator" and "Loser," and once again you cannot disagree.

Suddenly, you don't like yourself very much.

Then he pulls out his PowerPoint presentation and in full-color reveals every other area of poverty in your life. Your rejections, your betrayals, your lack of potential, your wrinkles, your unloveability, your bad habits, your busy itinerary, and your dead ends. And he will conclude his talk with several crushing blows so that you have no one to blame but yourself: "This is your life. The one that you chose. You don't have what you want to have. You don't do what you want to do. And you are not who you want to be." And you have to nod your head in shame. "I chose this paltry life. I did it to myself."

(Radiohead's *Just* plays in the background).

Suddenly, you dread everything about the coming lifetime. You despise the thought of every future Monday through Friday and you would like to change it all. But Satan presses a pillow over your desire and says: "It is too late. You cannot change. You are stuck. You are trapped. You have no choices. How it feels today is how it will feel from now on until you die. Now shut your mouth, put your shoes on, and march."

And with that set of lies, all positive thinking goes out of the window. Joel Osteen gets sacrificed on the kitchen counter. Faith in an Abundant Life becomes the silly talk of a balding guy in a Sunday morning robe. The Bible becomes comic book anti-reality. Jesus' assurance for the good life must have been a misquote. All of the promises of God are not Yes or even Maybe. According to our enemy, these promises are all No, No, No.

We know what Satan wants us to know. We buy a pair of "Air Thomas Hobbes" and slide them onto our souls. Life is nasty, brutish, and way too long. A six-pack of Heineken is as high as we are going to get.

The Eagles have landed.

Many Christians I know are experiencing this sort of existence—waking up most mornings listening to an interpretation of life that not only keeps them from climbing into the heavens, but which makes them wonder if they even have the ability to climb out of bed.

I have most certainly been there. I have experienced "down in the bed" dread. I walked around on eagle's feet for years. Hiding alcohol in corners of the pantry, "borrowing" hydrocodone, and overdrinking Red Bull to get some sort of liftoff. I tuned into the enemy's talk show until I memorized it and then turned it into an hourly replay that kept me from accepting the truth of God. Hating myself for choosing the life I was sure I could not change.

But recently, with my head bowed down in a defeated prayer position, I had my eyes opened. I noticed what appeared to be workable wings on each side of my body. And I heard a different voice—this one from God—saying, "Look in my Word and Listen to me about you."

So, I opened the Bible and asked the Spirit to speak to me about it. I changed the station and it changed my life. I put my eyes on the truth and the truth pulled my shoes off.

What is true?

This is the day that the Lord has made. I am not stuck. I am free to make changes. I am deeply loved. I am accepted. I am fearfully and wonderfully made. I will soar today. Nothing is impossible. I am not condemned. I am completely forgiven. God has got my back. God is looking to prosper me. God gives me good and perfect gifts. I have been given authority over my enemies. God is for me and no one can be against me. I have a God-given purpose. God is transforming me and completing me. I am a new creation. I am a temple of the Holy Spirit. Jesus has the keys to every one of my prisons. I am not forsaken. I am not alone.

I stand in front of a mirror most every day and say this stuff to myself. Things are not so bad. There is reason to hope.

I am like Stuart Smalley trying to re-program my inside mix-tape—trying to talk above the lying voices in my head.

Speaking out truth and affirmations that keep me out of daily therapy. I have yet to soar. But I have recently begun to hover.

Q & A

—What sorts of lies does Satan use to bring you down? To make you feel like a loser? To keep you grounded?

—What sort of "proof" does the enemy use to back up his lies so that you are more likely to believe him?

—What can you do to combat the lies? What do you currently do? How can a community of believers help you rise above the junk that is thrown at your mind?

—Do you allow Satan's claims to lead you towards self-hate and/or self-loathing?

—Describe yourself to your small group using the first five adjectives that pop into your head.

—Are you really hard on yourself? About what specific things? Do you ever beat up on yourself with negative self-talk? How do you think God sees you? How do you think God would want you to speak to yourself?

—What do you think Jesus meant by promising us an abundant and full life? What should our expectations be while on this earth regarding this promise?

—How do you think the truth of the Bible might help you combat the lies?

The Short Path

In Exodus 13:17, we read that God did not send the Israelites on the shortest route to the Promised Land.

Why?

Because God *knew something* about the Israelites. He knew that if these people faced Philistine opposition, they might choose to go back to Egypt. He knew that they would rather return to slavery than struggle with war. So the Israelites went the long way, and most of them never tasted the milk and honey.

Now I have to say that I want to be in God's Promised Land. I also have to say that I want to be there as fast as possible. *But what does God know about me?* Does He know something that will force Him to send me the long way? Am I so afraid of opposition and warfare that I would return to my slavery if threats came? Do I have so little faith that God has to send me on the easier path?

Probably.

Or maybe I am giving myself too much credit. Maybe I am deceiving myself into thinking I am even that far along. Maybe what God *knows* about me is that I am still sitting in a Jacuzzi in Egypt, nursing the injuries that come from brick making. Maybe He *knows* I am just fine with slavery and unwilling to follow Him toward a better place.

Q & A

—Do you sense that God has ever chosen to send you on a longer path to reach a promised destination because He knew you would not be able to handle the short path?

—Are you on a journey toward something with God right now? What sort of slavery are you leaving behind and what sort of promise is out there for you?

—Having been a slave to sin for years, do you find that you still long for the days of Egypt? Do you have days that make you want to turn back? To settle for what you had?

—What are the hardest things you have to deal with when traveling on God's journeys?

The Hero Is Really A Traitor?

I love when I hear Conservative Christians talking about Daniel as a hero. Would they consider him a hero if he lived today? I doubt it. Probably more of a traitor. Think about the facts.

Daniel became second in charge for Nebuchadnezzar, and Nebuchadnezzar was the guy who had come over and wiped out Daniel's nation. He was the king who decimated Israel. Now imagine America's being taken over by a cruel butcher of a dictator—the kind of guy who throws people into huge fires for no good reason. Now imagine an American male taking a job with this person and serving him and his rival nation—not as a spy bent on overthrow but as a loyal associate dedicated to helping.

What would you think about that?

I doubt you would call a man a hero who took a job with the leader who killed your friends and neighbors and destroyed Democracy. And I doubt you would believe him if he told you that God not only placed him in this employment, but that God was the one who gave the dictator his job.

But in the case of Daniel, that is basically what happened.

What should this tell you?

God is not easy to pin down. He is not so clear-cut. And He does not put up with any nation—even if it is full of His chosen people—if that nation chooses to rebel. And this puts America in the firing line. Yes. I said it. With our record of rebellion, we could very well get broken down by God at the hands of an evil nation.

Gasp.

Gasp.

Could this happen? It did to Israel, even though they supposed like most nations do, that it could not happen. And this destruction was by a leader much more evil than Bin Laden. And it was approved by God.

And one more thing to note: God might call you to do the oddest thing or ask you to take the strangest sort of job. He might even make you into a servant of the greatest enemy imaginable.

You never know.

Q & A

—Do you think Daniel had some good reasons to complain about his new Babylonian boss, Nebuchadnezzar? Give some examples.

—How do you think Daniel was able to be the best possible administrator for an "enemy" government that had destroyed his beloved Jerusalem?

—What should we learn about doing our best even in situations that do not seem fair?

—Has God ever placed you into a situation where you had to work hard for someone who was anti-Christian? For someone who acted in really ungodly ways? How did you handle that? If it happens in the future, how do you think you should handle it?

—How do you think today's media would treat someone like Daniel, who faithfully did what God wanted, but who also became a major resource for a national enemy? How would you think of him?

—Do you tend to judge people's actions in black and white ways, or do you leave room for God to do something totally weird and shocking?

—Can you think of another example of God's asking someone to do something that totally goes against what makes sense to you? (Hint: Abraham and Isaac) What does this say about God and your common sense?

—What would be a personal command from God that would shock you and make you hesitate to obey? What if he asked you to renounce your American citizenship and all the rights it affords to become a "person without a country?"

Jesus is the Reason for the Treason

Question: Is the Lord's Prayer treasonous?

In other words, when Jesus teaches His closest followers to pray, isn't he encouraging at least anti-patriotism?

Have you ever thought about the words you are praying when you say that common prayer—consider these:

"Our Father Who is in Heaven, hallowed be thy name. Your Kingdom come, Your will be done, on earth as it is in Heaven."

If I were Homeland Security, I would keep an eye on anyone who spoke those words.

Why?

Because that dangerous pray-er is calling on God to rule as the sovereign—not just in Heaven—but on this earth. It is a call for the immediate overthrow of human power and human systems. His "Kingdom come" does not mean we are asking for a nice merge of His system with Democracy and Capitalism. It is saying that we want Him to be the government and the governor and the policy maker over and against the system we live within.

It is asking the most powerful Being in the universe to come down and replace our President, our Congress, and our Judicial system—to change the way we go about living.

It is a reminder to ourselves and those around us that we do not prefer it here. We prefer it there. And we prefer "there" to "here" so much that we want "here" to be taken over by "there" ASAP.

With those words we recall that we are not citizens of any system on this planet—we are citizens of another empire altogether, One with a flag blood red that makes us boldly white when we salute it.

The Lord's Prayer is why I do not put my hand over my heart when the National Anthem plays. It is why I don't have an American flag waving in my front yard. The Lord's Prayer is why I do not stop at red lights (kidding).

I have a Kingdom and a King and I am loudly calling out for Him when I pray that prayer because I know He is the only Being who can satisfy me.

You have a kingdom, too.

Are you daring enough to call out for it and no other?

I'm not asking for a fight here. Not trying to rankle anyone with my interpretations. Really just trying to encourage all of us to KNOW that we are part of the BEST Empire and belong to the BEST Leader already.

So when the world disappoints you, don't bother mourning it as if it were supposed to lift you to the clouds, fix your eyes on who He has made you to be—A world-weary alien and a stranger who groans for the next world.

With love and treason from your fellow alien,

BD

Q & A

—Do you really believe in what the Lord's Prayer is all about? Or do you pretty much just say it because you always have?

—How can each line of that prayer become more powerful to you? How can this prayer become meaningful in your life?

—Why do you think Jesus told his followers to pray this way?

—What is the significance of calling on God to replace your own government? What does your opinion say about you?

—Would you rather have your way or God's way if they were in conflict? Be honest!

The Post-Good Church

(This chapter is not aimed at the many churches that are really seeking God for the right reasons and not business reasons. It is also not aimed at church leaders who are throwing themselves into prayer, obedience and surrender so that God can be glorified within the flocks they have been given to pastor. But, this chapter *is aimed* at those "locations" that hang a "church" sign outside and make a good go at financial growth and power jumps with a slick, topical, and relevant show.)

Are most church services set up to be self-serving infomercials?

Are we serving up a $19.99 Jesus to an audience who sings and claps and gets a warm-up for a tough week? The excited host showing off how many cool things Christianity has to offer. Paid advertisements—like beggars hoping the crowd won't leave them empty-handed.

"We depend on your purchase of my sermon. We depend on your purchase of our songs. We pay our house payments and our car payments because you seize our version of the deal. We think most of you are lazy complainers. We talk bad about a lot of you behind your backs because you do not do the things we want. You are sucky disciples. You like committees. We put up with them.

But when we see you pile into chairs before us on a week-to-week basis, we put on the show of a lifetime. We even stick passed plates in your hands and dare you not to put anything in. Buy, Buy, Buy. You control our destiny."

By the way, I do not believe in the term post-modern. I do not think that this is the problem in the church today—the problem that speakers and writers are trying to solve for the health of the church. The issue that the church needs to deal with is post-good—or should I say post-God. Never in my life did I think that Nietzsche's quote, "God is dead/unnecessary," would ever apply to a lot of congregations, but I have seen it again and again.

We use God often as a brand—maybe even a franchise—one that beams His name in neon lights and yet serves up a ridiculous version of some strange Savior and Lord once you sit down at the table.

"Excuse me, waiter/pastor—is this the Jesus I ordered?"

"Of course, sir."

"It tastes weird."

"That's because we added high fructose corn syrup to His mixture so He tastes more like you are used to. Would you prefer your Jesus to be gluten-free? We can do that too."

Post-good churches.

Once again, I encourage you to read the letters to the churches in the book of Revelation.

Find good.

Do better.

Q & A

—What is your opinion about the current state of the Western Church?

—How would you say that your own church gathering compares to the average church gathering in the West?

—If you could determine a set of essentials that a spiritual gathering would have to follow to be allowed to claim the name and non-profit status of a "church," what would some of those essentials be?

Jesus Doesn't Want a Gym

Remember back in early AD, after Jesus dunked that basketball over the heads of the Pharisees in the new Family Life Gym in Samaria, he said to his disciples, "I posterize thee in the name of Michael Jordan."

That was funny stuff by Jesus.

And remember how he took that one green bean casserole from the elderly lady and fed the five thousand members of his denomination in the new Family Life Center's Banquet Hall. It gave me chills when he broke that Tupperware container in two and distributed its contents so that all of the people were full. Then when he said, "Isn't it cool that we have such an amazing new building to have potlucks in," I knew right then that we had made the right decision to use up thousands of hours of time and millions of dollars on this space.

Down with Family Life Centers:

I almost got fired/forced to resign for this issue at church I once worked for. A new head pastor (whom I appreciate personally) had been brought in to help excite the masses at this extremely traditional downtown church. He was here to make sure this "much needed" building project went forward, and I was one of the very few not going for it. I could not imagine how this glorified gymnasium with new places for the youth to play and with spaces for grand lunches to be held could be the will of God. Our church was located in an economically lower class area that had a growing homeless population but no shelter yet built in the city. A homeless shelter was needed, and if anyone could have led a successful charge for such a facility, our church could have been the one to do it. We were filled with power, riches, and politicians who could combine their blessings with their compassionate Christianity to make sure kids and families and humans down on their luck could have a safe bed for several nights—and possibly even a long term rehab program to help people come back from the dead. But that didn't cross the minds of our leaders. We had a soup kitchen, a bare bones benevolence budget, and that was enough. Whether I liked it or not, it was going to be ten million dollars for a basketball court, nice showers, some swankier offices, and a state-of-the-art youth space.

That was first priority.

Why?

Because we needed to attract more people to our church. Other downtown churches had built sweet gyms and sweet places to hold ping-pong and domino tournaments, and they were growing. They were bursting at the seams while we were losing people. Also, the city as a whole was relocating itself to the southwest of us—new developments and new churches springing up in those new developments were taking our members. Our current members were saying, "Why drive 20 minutes downtown on a Sunday morning where a homeless guy might sit next to me on the pew, when I can just walk down the street and get a sermon of equal quality and no threat of heterogeneity?"

That was our biggest problem—desertion for the sake of convenience. We knew the stories of how once prestigious downtown churches in other cities had collapsed due to similar circumstances. We had to do something before it was too late. The Baptists had. The Church of Christ had. The Nazarenes had. We had not. So, we needed something that was going to say to everyone in town: "Hey, we are the best. We are the church with the most amenities. We are a five-star holy ground. You don't just get Jesus here—you get Jesus plus hoops. You get God plus valet parking. You get the Holy Spirit plus a country club." It made sense to them. And so that is what they did. It didn't seem to be a decision motivated by prayer as much as it was by good business planning, which might be the very opposite of faith in this world, but it was happening.

And from the moment the project was approved, there was a shift in our priorities. All we talked about at staff meetings was how we were going to raise the money for this deal. I have never seen so much guilt/inspirational marketing in my life. Every Bible story dealing with sacrificial giving was preached ad nauseum. The widow must have given her last mite a hundred times. House meetings that gathered up the rich into "sweat 'em out" pitch sessions happened—people vying to name chalices, crosses, prayer chapels after themselves became common. It got ugly. People quit donating as much to missions and were giving cash for named bricks.

And anyone who had an opposite opinion was shunned.

I could not remain in such a place. I left soon after telling the pastor what I thought of the choice to build such a masterpiece over and above a place where the needy and hurting could be helped. I told him that such a decision would be met with judgment. At least I hoped it would.

Right now, the beautiful building is finished and there is still not even close to enough shelter in my city. But there will surely be more competitive basketball leagues and definitely more competition among churches trying to capture the solid-giving members.

Beyond my personal church experience, I just cannot wrap my head around the purpose of these Centers. I do not think God ever had in mind this sort of expansion. Can you imagine the Temple in Jerusalem with a Family Life Center attached? I think Jesus would have pulled down the rims, cut down the nets, and dribbled himself right out of their midst.

I am wondering—when will we figure out that people are not supposed to come to church mainly to have fun? Churches were created so that people can be discipled and sent out. We do not need to develop an amenity-based church that will get people into our back doors so that we can then evangelize them. Front door spiritual evangelism is the best bet. If the members of your churches are full of the Spirit and bearing fruit on a daily basis, then you do not need a gym to recruit new people. People will come because God is inside your place. God will be your publicity. He is what sets a church apart from a YMCA.

Last thought: while it is true that if you build it, they may come, it is also true that God may leave.

Q & A

—What do you think drives church leadership groups to build amenity-based buildings to attract larger populations?

—How do you feel about giving to a Capital Campaign? Ever been a part of one?

—While on the topic of giving, what does the New Testament say about Gentiles tithing their income?

—How should churches determine their level of success? What is the proper measure for deciding whether a church is one of God's top-notch ministries?

—Why would you say that church attendance all over the nation is in decline? What advice would you give to a church that is seeking to grow? How would you consult them? What steps should they take?

—Is bigger, cooler, and newer always better?

—How has competition between churches hurt God's vision for unity among the Body? How do you think unbelievers feel about what they see going on with churches?

—If you were an unbeliever, do you think having access to a gym and a family life center would get you to come to church? Do you think it would in any way be a catalyst for your conversion or your growth as a Christian?

Viva Las Jesus

Two quick things:

> -Vegas is not Sin City. Sin City is actually whatever city humans live in.

> -There are parts of Vegas that I like. It feels like another planet, which is good when you are sick of the planet you live on.

Go ahead and judge. That's fine with me. You go on and hang in a Starbucks in the middle of a National Park and read those Christian Romance novels for your vacation. I am hitting the Strip. Bible Study in the morning, Texas Hold 'Em in the afternoon.

Okay, so yes, I am about to go on a vacation to Las Vegas and for a week now, the anticipation has taken over. I keep having dreams of catching that $750 million nickel slot progressive, feeling wealthy and free, busting up big poker games, hitting red twenty times straight, getting my wife and me comped into the penthouse suite at Bellagio with unlimited spa services, and getting the ultimate escape.

Swimming pools and Jacuzzi bathtubs and clove cigarettes and anonymity and no church work.

Worldliness. Sweet Worldliness.

But then God ruined it for me—or maybe He just cleared it up for me: Las Vegas is not going to make me happy. It never does. The guy to my left will always have quad aces when I have a full house. You don't get penthouse comped for playing nickel slots. The pools are urinated in. The vacation is temporary. Whatever happens there, stays there. You cannot take the escape home with you.

Vegas is always a depressing trick. Full of false hopes.

I am realizing that if I cannot find joy in the eternal and faithful and loving and rich God before I go, I am a moron. Jesus has a better voice than Celine Dion. Jesus has more interesting moves than Cirque De Soleil.

Jesus has the best penthouse prepared for me.

So, Viva Las Jesus.

I am going to learn to enjoy life right where I am.

May His Kingdom come.

I am betting on it.

Q & A

—Ever been to Las Vegas? What are your impressions of it?

—Do you have any Vegas rules you make sure to follow so that you don't get swallowed up by the temptations?

—Is there anything tempting about Vegas to you? What are the most dangerous parts of its offerings?

—Any serious Vegas regrets that need confessing or that caused damage in your life?

—How do you think God views the city of Las Vegas? How do you think He wants His people to view it?

—How has the Sodom mindset infiltrated every part of our society? Your city? Your home? What can be done to stop it?

—Do you tend to justify "escapes" that are sinful and/or unhealthy?

The Kingdom of God: A Final Stream of Consciousness

The New Kingdom is again capturing my thought. When Jesus taught, he mainly spoke of the Kingdom to come—not about how to squeak by or successfully thrive in the kingdoms that are all around us.

First question is who gets in? Who is going to be in this wonderful New Earth? Who is in the book? Who is blotted out?

Second thing I consider is just how different this system will be under God:

The governance will not be democratic.

The currency will not be dollars.

The relationships will not be marital.

Shopping will be unnecessary.

Televisions will not be present.

Businesses are not important.

How we spend time there will be radically different.

I wonder how.

Do sports happen?

Does sex happen?

Do we sleep?

Clothing?

Will there be boredom?

Will there be need for diversion?

Equality reigns, doesn't it?

No worry about building your body when you have a glorious one, right?

It's the unblurry God living alongside us in a clear world.

Incredible places prepared.

Places of love.

No worry.

No fear.

Beauty all around.

No depression.

No sadness.

No rush.

No holidays.

No need for weekends or vacations.

No drunkenness.

No drugs.

But there will be parties.

And there will be a bunch of angels.

Sin and all of its causes/causers will be gone.

No need for schools or educational facilities.

Pure Understanding and Wisdom.

No computers.

No corporations.

No supply and demand.

No insecurities.

Will this whole new system freak us out?

How does someone prepare for it? Seems like a blind man's being told he is about to see for the first time—can you imagine his imaginations? His appreciations? His excitements?

No politics and no politicians.

No thieves.

No pain.

Will it feel like the most wonderful victory at all times?

Lifetime outsiders becoming first-class citizens.

Not getting caught up in what does not matter.

Will there be such an internal re-creation that we could care less about technology and already feel the best-ness of the new? I imagine that comes with the glory of our bodies...

I know I watch my four-year-old nephew care about toys I could absolutely care less about. He loves them and is totally fascinated by them, but it is just a stage. He will also care less about them in time. He will care about cooler things, more advanced things. And since God is the most advanced Creator, I can only imagine what He has in store for us.

Do you know what it is like to be consumed by the Holy Spirit—even for an hour? Even for a minute? That sense of connection intellectually and emotionally is stronger than any drug I have ever had—a lot stronger. It is possessive and powerful and you long to remain in it and do nothing else but be inside of it...

So if the new system allows for that I would gladly trade in all things—every device and diversion that has been thrown at me, every bowl of soup, for a constant connection in the Holy Spirit to God.

The sense of absolute closeness and belonging is the best.

It is warm and waves and love and peace, and I'll bet you it is only a taste of what it feels like to be in the presence of God.

Those who do not have Jesus as Lord are going to miss out on the new system—all they will have known is how to function within a very, very imperfect system.

So, success on earth—worldly success—isn't it just figuring out how to slide through passages showing various cards and retina scans—based on talent and relationships and using trickery ambition and sometimes even dubious ladders to climb?

Can God place a person at the top? Sure. But it is not like you are going to learn much of value there. You might impact those on top, but it is more likely that you will be infected and polluted.

Who cares if you do well on this planet in worldly terms?

To love and encourage others and to have certainty in the coming of the One—that is the job of the alien.

Well Done, Good and Faithful.

Are you tired of the world's best attempts to drive you?

I love how Ecclesiastes 3 puts it. Sure, there is a time for every-thing—but it does not really matter. Earth is a lot of busywork, and we cannot see well enough to notice God's beauty.

Elisha had vision. He could see the spiritual. God allows us that pleasure, too, in dreams and visions. May the Spirit of the Holy God show you what you have yet to see.

Q & A

—Are you aware daily of the coming Kingdom of God?

—How do considerations of the Kingdom of God drive your decisions in the everyday?

—How do you let yourself get caught up in the world that is passing away?

—How can you stop yourself from loving and believing in the systems of this world?

—Why do you think we have created such a different looking system in this world? Why have we not aimed to develop a more "Kingdom Culture?"

—How much does your church or life group talk about/plan for the development of a more "Kingdom Culture?"

—What do you think would be the hardest adjustment for you if you began to live a more Kingdom-centered existence? What would have to change?

Conclusion: Stop talking!

Okay, the dialogues are over. Thanks for allowing me to invade your minds with my ideas that are based on limited experiences but on unlimited wisdom.

And thanks for taking the questions seriously. Questions are the key to new discovery, and I hope you got into some deep discovery discussions with your mates while grabbing onto God's forceful Kingdom movement as you talked.

But now the time for talking is over as we all step into the world with a few new things to apply.

This book was not written to turn you into a critic, but into a change agent within the systems around you. So, be transformed in the Spirit and then go be a transformer with God's zeal and His knowledge. He has things set up for you to do.

Put the book down and go find your set-ups. Grace and Peace to you as you roll out The New Christian Whatever in the real world.

www.ingramcontent.com/pod-product-compliance
Lightning Source LLC
LaVergne TN
LVHW051248080426
835513LV00016B/1812